SMOOTHIES
AND SHAKES

SMOOTHIES
AND SHAKES

30 HEAVENLY BLENDS SHOWN IN 60 DELICIOUS PHOTOGRAPHS

Susannah Blake

southwater

PUBLISHER: Joanna Lorenz
MANAGING EDITOR: Linda Fraser
PROJECT EDITOR: Susannah Blake
DESIGNER: Anita Schnable
PHOTOGRAPHY: Steve Baxter, Martin Brigdale, Gus Filgate, Amanda Heywood, Janine Hosegood, William Lindwood, and Craig Robertson
RECIPES: Susannah Blake, Matthew Drennan, Nicola Graimes, Sara Lewis and Oona van den Berg

ETHICAL TRADING POLICY

Because of our ongoing ecological investment programme, you, as our customer, can have the pleasure and reassurance of knowing that a tree is being cultivated on your behalf to naturally replace the materials used to make the book you are holding. For further information about this scheme, go to www.annesspublishing.com/trees

A CIP catalogue record for this book is available from the British Library.

NOTES

Bracketed terms are intended for American readers.

For all recipes, quantities are given in both metric and imperial measures and, where appropriate, in standard cups and spoons. Follow one set of measures, but not a mixture, because they are not interchangeable.

Standard spoon and cup measures are level. 1 tsp = 5ml, 1 tbsp = 15ml, 1 cup = 250ml/8fl oz.

Australian standard tablespoons are 20ml. Australian readers should use 3 tsp in place of 1 tbsp for measuring small quantities.

American pints are 16fl oz/2 cups. American readers should use 20fl oz/2.5 cups in place of 1 pint when measuring liquids.

Previously published as *Smoothies: Blended Drinks and Health Juices*

This edition is published by Southwater, an imprint of Anness Publishing Ltd, Hermes House, 88–89 Blackfriars Road, London SE1 8HA; tel. 020 7401 2077; fax 020 7633 9499

www.southwaterbooks.com; www.annesspublishing.com

If you like the images in this book and would like to investigate using them for publishing, promotions or advertising, please visit our website www.practicalpictures.com for more information.

UK agent: The Manning Partnership Ltd;
tel. 01225 478444; fax 01225 478440;
sales@manning-partnership.co.uk
UK distributor: Grantham Book Services Ltd;
tel. 01476 541080; fax 01476 541061; orders@gbs.tbs-ltd.co.uk
North American agent/distributor: National Book Network;
tel. 301 459 3366; fax 301 429 5746; www.nbnbooks.com
Australian agent/distributor: Pan Macmillan Australia;
tel. 1300 135 113; fax 1300 135 103;
customer.service@macmillan.com.au
New Zealand agent/distributor: David Bateman Ltd;
tel. (09) 415 7664; fax (09) 415 8892

contents

making smoothies, blended drinks and health juices

Many different kinds of blended drinks can be made quickly and easily with the help of a food processor, blender or juice extractor. Fruit can be blended with yogurt, milk or juice to create a classic smoothie, or juiced with vegetables for a feel-good health shot. A smoothie or juice can be turned into a thick, creamy shake by blending with a scoop or two of ice cream. Alternatively, blending them with crushed ice will make a delicious low-calorie frozen drink.

classic smoothies

These simple drinks are usually a combination of soft-textured fruits, such as strawberries or peaches, blended with milk or yogurt. They can be thick or thin, refreshing or filling, and either sweet or savoury. There are lots of variations on the classic smoothie. For example, fruit juice, coconut milk or soya milk can be used in place of milk or yogurt.

making a basic fruit smoothie

For the best results, you will need a food processor or blender.

1 Choose a soft-textured fruit or a combination of fruits, such as banana and mango, raspberry and peach or pineapple and papaya.

2 Peel, stone (pit) or hull 250g/9oz/ about 1½ cups fruit and cut the flesh into large chunks.

3 Place the fruit in a food processor or blender and add 120ml/4fl oz/ ½ cup yogurt and 120ml/4fl oz/ ½ cup milk. Process for 1–2 minutes until smooth and frothy, then pour into a glass and serve.

To make a smoothie without a food processor, place soft-textured fruit, such as raspberries or strawberries, in a bowl and mash with a fork, then press through a sieve into a large jug (pitcher). Add the milk and yogurt and whisk until frothy.

fruit and vegetable juices

Hard and soft fruits and vegetables, leafy greens and fresh herbs can all be enjoyed as delicious juices. For the best results, you will need a juice extractor that first pulps the fruit and vegetables, them removes the juice. To obtain optimum nutritional benefits, drink these juices straight away.

making pure juices

To make these, you will need a juice extractor that can juice hard and soft fruits and vegetables, leafy greens and peeled citrus fruits.

1 Choose a combination of fruits and vegetables, such as pear and melon, carrot and apple, or tomato, celery and cucumber.

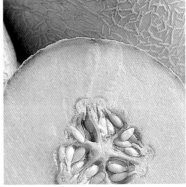

2 Different fruits and vegetables contain varying amounts of juice; adjust quantities according to the ingredients. As a guide, prepare about 300g/11oz/2½ cups of the fruit and/or vegetables: scrub vegetables (trimming them if necessary), stone (pit) fruit and remove any thick peel.

3 Cut the fruit and/or vegetables into large chunks and use a juice extractor to juice. Serve immediately.

icy blends

Add ice cream or ice to a basic smoothie or juice to create delicious, thick, frozen drinks that are perfect for summer.

making frozen drinks with ice cream

You will need a food processor or blender to make ice cream smoothies and shakes.

1 Place 250g/9oz/1–1½ cups soft fruit, such as blueberries, into a food processor or blender. Pour in 175ml/6fl oz/¾ cup skimmed milk and add 2–3 scoops of ice cream. Process briefly until well mixed and smooth. Serve immediately.

making frozen drinks with ice

You will need a powerful blender that can crush ice.

making thick blended juices

If you do not own a juice extractor, you can make fruit juices in a food processor or blender. Blended juices tend to be thicker than regular juices and have a higher fibre content because the pulp has not been removed. Soft, juicy fruits, such as melon, pear and grapes, are all ideal for blended juices.

1 Choose one fruit or combination of fruits, such as melon and grape.

2 Peel, stone (pit), core or seed the fruit, cut the flesh into chunks and place in a food processor or blender. With fruit such as melon, it is easier to remove the seeds and scoop the flesh out of the skin straight into the food processor or blender.

3 Process the fruit for 2–3 minutes until very smooth. If the juice is very thick, add a little water or fruit juice and process to combine. Pour into a glass and serve immediately.

1 Wrap 125ml/8fl oz/1 cup ice cubes in a dishtowel and smash with a wooden mallet to break into smaller pieces. Place in a blender.

2 Add 250g/9oz/1–1½ cups soft fruit, such as raspberries, to the blender and pour in 120ml/4fl oz/½ cup fruit juice, such as orange juice. Blend for 2–3 minutes, or until the ice is finely crushed and the ingredients are combined. Pour into a glass and serve immediately.

flavouring smoothies and juices

Additional flavourings can be added to a basic smoothie or juice mix to enhance the flavours and create even more delicious combinations.

Honey and flavoured syrups, such as maple syrup or ginger syrup, will add sweetness and flavour to smoothies and juices. Make the drink, then blend in a little honey or syrup to taste.

Aromatic spices such as ginger, cinnamon and vanilla make a good addition to fruity blends. Add a pinch of ground spice to a smoothie or juice. Alternatively, make a spice syrup by infusing whole spices, such as cinnamon or vanilla, in a little water and sugar. Fresh spices, such as ginger, should be grated.

Fresh herbs can enhance the natural flavours of fruit and vegetable juices. Blend a few mint or lemon balm leaves with fruity mixtures, such as melon, pear and grape, or add coriander (cilantro), parsley or basil to vegetable mixtures, such as carrot and celery juice.

For extra bite, a little finely chopped fresh chilli can make a wonderful, peppery addition to both sweet and savoury blended drinks, while garlic can complement the flavours of a vegetable juice.

Coffee and chocolate can be used to flavour milky drinks. Blend a cooled espresso or a little chocolate syrup with milk and ice, or to make a frozen drink blend together coffee or chocolate ice cream and milk.

Liqueurs and spirits can give extra punch to blended drinks. Try peach schnapps with fruit drinks or add clear spirits such as vodka to vegetable juices. More full-bodied spirits, such as brandy or tequila, make a good addition to both fruit- and vegetable-based drinks.

smoothies and shakes

Thick and creamy shakes and smoothies are delicious at any time of day, whether as a nutritious breakfast or a mid-afternoon treat. This chapter includes an enticing selection of wonderful recipes, from simple, healthy smoothies made with fresh fruit, milk and yogurt, to more daring and unusual combinations such as avocado and lime smoothie with green chilli salsa.

banana-passion shake

This wonderfully frothy shake is surprisingly refreshing. Sparkling mineral water gives a light touch to the creamy blend of banana and yogurt while passion fruit adds a subtle tang.

1 Cut the banana into rough chunks and place in a food processor or blender. Cut the passion fruits in half and scoop the flesh and seeds into a fine sieve. Using the back of a spoon, press the flesh through the sieve into the food processor or blender.

2 Add the yogurt to the food processor or blender and process for 2 minutes until very smooth and frothy.

3 Pour the shake into two tall glasses, then pour on the sparkling water. Sprinkle with a little nutmeg, if you like, and serve immediately.

1 ripe banana, peeled
2 passion fruits
150ml/¼ pint/⅔ cup natural (plain) yogurt
100ml/3½fl oz/generous ⅓ cup sparkling
    mineral water
grated nutmeg, to sprinkle (optional)

Serves 2

Variation
To make a mango-passion shake, use a small, very ripe, peeled, stoned (pitted) and chopped mango in place of the banana.

raspberry and orange smoothie

This exquisite blend combines the sharp-sweet taste of raspberries and oranges with the light creaminess of yogurt. It takes just minutes to prepare, making it perfect for breakfast — or any other time of the day.

250g/9oz/1⅓ cups raspberries, chilled
200ml/7fl oz/scant 1 cup natural (plain) yogurt, chilled
300ml/½ pint/1¼ cups freshly squeezed orange juice, chilled

Serves 2–3

1 Place the raspberries and yogurt in a food processor or blender and process for about 1 minute until smooth and creamy.

2 Add the orange juice to the raspberry and yogurt mixture and process for about 30 seconds, or until thoroughly combined. Pour into tall glasses and serve immediately.

Cook's Tip
For a super-chilled version, use frozen raspberries instead of fresh. You may need to blend the raspberries and yogurt for a little longer to get a really smooth result.

strawberry, banana
and coconut smoothie

The blend of perfectly ripe bananas and creamed coconut gives this decadently thick and creamy combination its velvety smooth taste and texture.

1 Hull the strawberries. Peel the bananas and cut them into rough chunks.

2 Put the fruit in a food processor or blender, crumble in the coconut and add the water. Process until smooth, scraping down the sides of the goblet as necessary.

3 Add the skimmed milk, lemon juice and ice cubes, crushing the ice first unless you have a heavy-duty processor. Process until smooth and thick. Pour into tall glasses and top each with a slice or two of strawberry. Serve immediately.

200g/7oz/1¾ cups strawberries, plus extra, sliced, to decorate
2 ripe bananas
115g/4oz creamed coconut (coconut cream)
120ml/4fl oz/½ cup water
175ml/6fl oz/¾ cup skimmed (skim) milk
30ml/2 tbsp lemon juice
10 ice cubes

Serves 4

Variations
• To give this smoothie a tropical flavour, use papaya, mango or pineapple in place of the strawberries and add lime juice rather than lemon.
• To make a dairy-free version, replace the skimmed milk with soya milk.

avocado and lime
smoothie with green chilli salsa

Inspired by guacamole, this wonderfully thick and creamy smoothie combines mild and spicy flavours perfectly.

1 Prepare the salsa first. Mix all the ingredients and season to taste with salt and pepper. Chill while you prepare the smoothie.

2 Halve and stone (pit) the avocados. Scoop out the flesh and place in a blender that can crush ice. Add the lime juice, garlic, ice cubes and about 150ml/¼ pint/⅔ cup of the vegetable stock and process until smooth.

3 Pour the mixture into a large jug (pitcher) and stir in the remaining stock, milk, sour cream, Tabasco and seasoning.

4 Pour the smoothie into 4 glasses and spoon a little salsa on to each. Add a splash of olive oil to each portion and garnish with fresh coriander leaves. Serve immediately – with a spoon.

3 ripe avocados
juice of 1½ limes
1 garlic clove, crushed
handful of ice cubes
400ml/14fl oz/1⅔ cups vegetable
    stock, chilled
400ml/14fl oz/1⅔ cups milk, chilled
150ml/¼ pint/⅔ cup sour cream, chilled
few drops of Tabasco sauce
salt and ground black pepper
fresh coriander (cilantro) leaves, to garnish
extra virgin olive oil, to serve

For the salsa
4 tomatoes, peeled, seeded and finely diced
2 spring onions (scallions), finely chopped
1 green chilli, seeded and finely chopped
15ml/1 tbsp chopped fresh coriander (cilantro)
juice of ½ lime
salt and ground black pepper

Serves 4

liquid therapy

The healing powers of fruits and vegetables are quite astounding. They are all packed with nutrients and phytochemicals that can help to ward off ill-health, heal the body and boost your vital organs. Fresh juices brim with goodness and offer a delicious, natural medicine. Whether you want to cleanse your body, revitalize your spirit or calm your system, this chapter is sure to offer the perfect juice blend.

apple and leaf lift-off

This delicious blend of apple, grapes, fresh leaves and lime juice is the perfect rejuvenator and is great for treating skin, liver and kidney disorders.

1 Quarter the apple. Using a juice extractor, juice the fruit, coriander and watercress or rocket.

2 Add the lime juice to the fruit and herb mixture and stir. Pour into a tall glass and serve immediately.

1 apple
150g/5oz white grapes
small handful of fresh coriander (cilantro),
   stalks included
25g/1oz watercress or rocket (arugula)
15ml/1 tbsp lime juice

Serves 1

fennel fusion

This hefty combination of raw vegetables and apples makes a surprisingly delicious juice. Cabbage has natural anti-bacterial properties, while apples and fennel can help to cleanse the system.

1 Roughly slice the cabbage and fennel and quarter the apples. Using a juice extractor, juice the vegetables and fruit.

2 Add the lemon juice to the juice mixture and stir. Pour into a glass and serve immediately.

½ small red cabbage
½ fennel bulb
2 apples
15ml/1 tbsp lemon juice

Serves 1

tropical calm

This deliciously scented juice is packed with the cancer-fighting antioxidant betacarotene and can aid liver and kidney function, which helps to cleanse the system.

1 Halve the papaya, remove the seeds and skin, then cut the flesh into rough slices. Halve the melon, remove the seeds, cut into quarters, slice the flesh away from the skin and cut into chunks.

2 Juice the fruit, using a juicer, or blend in a food processor or blender for a thicker juice, and serve immediately.

1 papaya
½ cantaloupe melon
90g/3½oz white grapes

Serves 1

strawberry soother

Relax with this comforting strawberry blend, which is rich in vitamin C and healing phytochemicals.

1 Hull the strawberries, then quarter the peach or nectarine and pull out the stone (pit). Cut the flesh into rough slices or chunks.

2 Juice the fruit, using a juicer, or blend in a food processor or blender for a thicker juice, and serve immediately.

225g/8oz/2 cups
    strawberries
1 peach or nectarine

Serves 1

pineapple protector

This zingy yellow juice is the perfect pick-me-up at the end of a hard day with its boost of instant energy combined with pineapple's healing enzymes.

1 Peel the pineapples, remove the core and "eyes" and chop the flesh. Place in a food processor or blender and add the lime and grapefruit juice and half the water. Process to a pulp. Stop the machine and scrape the mixture from the sides once or twice.

2 Place a sieve over a large bowl. Tip the pineapple pulp into the sieve and press with the back of a wooden spoon to extract the juice. Pour the sieved mixture into a large jug (pitcher).

3 Stir in the remaining water and add sugar to taste. Pour into tall glasses and add one or two ice cubes to each. Serve immediately.

2 pineapples, chilled
juice of 2 limes
juice of ½ grapefruit
475ml/16fl oz/2 cups still mineral
    water, chilled
50g/2oz/¼ cup caster (superfine) sugar,
    to taste
ice cubes, to serve

Serves 4

honey and watermelon tonic

This refreshing juice will help to cool the body, calm the digestion and cleanse the system and may even have aphrodisiac qualities.

1 watermelon
1 litre/1¾ pints/4 cups chilled water
juice of 2 limes
clear honey, to taste
ice cubes, to serve

Serves 4

1 Cut the watermelon flesh into chunks, cutting away the skin and discarding the black seeds.

2 Place the watermelon chunks in a large bowl, pour the chilled water over and leave to stand for 10 minutes.

3 Tip the mixture into a large sieve set over a bowl. Using a wooden spoon, press gently on the fruit to extract all the liquid.

4 Stir in the lime juice and sweeten to taste with honey. Pour into a jug (pitcher), add ice cubes and stir. Serve in tall glasses.

carrot revitalizer

This vibrant fruit and vegetable combination will help to rejuvenate your body and soul with its dose of immune-boosting vitamin C, protective betacarotene and energizing natural fruit sugars.

1 Scrub and trim the carrots and quarter the apple. Peel the orange and cut into rough segments.

2 Using a juice extractor, juice the carrots and fruit, pour into a glass and serve immediately.

3 carrots
1 apple
1 orange

Serves 1

purple pep

This potent blend will not only help to kick-start your system — cleansing, nourishing and stimulating the body — it also offers a healthy dose of protective antioxidant nutrients.

1 Scrub and trim the carrots and beetroot and cut the beetroot into large chunks.

2 Using a juice extractor, juice all the vegetables, then pour into a glass and serve immediately.

3 carrots
115g/4oz beetroot (beet)
30g/1oz baby spinach, washed and dried
2 celery sticks

Serves 1

raw refreshment

Fresh and raw fruit and
vegetable juices offer the ultimate
in feel-good refreshment. Tantalize
your tastebuds with freshly-made
juices and feel your body tingle as
it absorbs those vital vitamins and
minerals. This wonderful selection
of fresh juice blends offers the
ultimate in health treats –
deliciously tempting but
wholesomely healthy.

power-booster

This energizing blend of fresh ginger, super-cleansing vegetables and natural fruit sugars is the perfect wake-up call for your body.

1 Quarter the apples and scrub and trim the carrot. Using a juice extractor, juice the fruit, vegetables and ginger, pour into a glass and serve immediately.

2 apples
90g/3½ oz white grapes
1 large carrot
50g/2oz cooked beetroot (beet) in
    natural juice
1cm/½in piece of fresh root ginger

Serves 1

veggie vigour

Perfectly ripe tomatoes and pungent garlic make a wonderful base for this ruby-red juice, which offers powerful protection for the body.

3 large, vine-ripened tomatoes, halved
½ Little Gem (Bibb) lettuce, halved
5cm/2in piece cucumber
1 small garlic clove
small handful of fresh parsley,
    stalks included
15ml/1 tbsp lemon juice

Serves 1

1 Peel and chop the cucumber. Using a juice extractor, juice all the ingredients, pour into a glass and serve immediately.

apple shiner

Enjoy radiant skin and instant energy with this cleansing fusion of apple, honeydew melon, red grapes and lemon.

1 Quarter the apple and remove the core. Cut the melon into quarters, remove the seeds and slice the flesh away from the skin.

2 Using a juice extractor, juice the fruit. Alternatively, process the fruit in a food processor or blender for 2–3 minutes until smooth. Pour the juice into a glass, stir in the lemon juice and serve.

1 apple
½ honeydew melon
90g/3½oz red grapes
15ml/1 tbsp lemon juice

Serves 1

melon pick-me-up

This spicy blend of melon, pear and fresh root ginger will revive your body, stimulate your circulation and fire you into action.

1 Quarter the melon, remove the seeds and slice the flesh away from the skin, then quarter the pears.

2 Using a juice extractor, juice all the ingredients, pour into a tall glass and serve immediately.

½ cantaloupe melon
2 pears
2.5cm/1in piece of fresh
    root ginger

Serves 1

hum-zinger

This tropical cleanser will help boost the digestive system and the kidneys, making your eyes sparkle, your hair shine and your skin glow.

1 Remove any "eyes" left in the pineapple, then cut all the fruit into rough chunks. Using a juice extractor, juice the fruit. Alternatively, use a food processor or blender and process for 2–3 minutes until very smooth. Pour into a glass and serve immediately.

½ pineapple, peeled
1 small mango, peeled and pitted
½ small papaya, seeded and peeled

Serves 1

citrus sparkle

Zesty citrus fruits are packed with immune-boosting vitamin C that can help to ward off winter colds and put a spring in your step.

1 Cut the grapefruit and orange in half and squeeze out the juice using a citrus fruit squeezer. Pour the juice into a glass, stir in the lemon juice and serve immediately.

1 pink grapefruit
1 orange
30ml/2 tbsp lemon juice

Serves 1

sunburst

This juice is packed with health-promoting phytochemicals and protective betacarotene, making it the perfect start to any day.

1 Place the apple, carrots and mango in a food processor or blender and process to a pulp. Add the orange juice and strawberries and process again.

2 Place a large sieve over a bowl and pour in the fruit pulp. Press out all the juice using the back of a wooden spoon. Discard any pulp left in the sieve.

3 Pour the juice into tall glasses filled with ice. Decorate each with a slice of orange and serve immediately.

1 green apple, cored and chopped
3 carrots, peeled and chopped
1 mango, peeled, and stoned (pitted)
150ml/¼ pint/⅔ cup freshly squeezed orange juice, chilled
6 strawberries, hulled
ice cubes, to serve
slices of orange, to decorate

Serves 2

Variation
To make a nutritious breakfast smoothie, blend half a glass of sunburst with half a glass of natural (plain) yogurt.

cold comfort

What could be more decadent than a drink thick with ice cream or crushed ice? Semi-frozen smoothies and shakes can be wonderfully cooling on a hot summer day and can even be considered a dessert and drink in one. Light and icy, thick and creamy or tangy with frozen yogurt – these frosty feasts are sure to delight.

cranberry, ginger and
cinnamon spritzer

Partially freezing fruit juice gives it a refreshing slushy texture. The combination of cranberry and apple juice adds a tart, clean flavour that's not too sweet.

1 Pour the cranberry juice into a shallow freezerproof container and freeze for about 2 hours or until a thick layer of ice crystals has formed around the edges.

2 Mash with a fork to break up the ice, then return the mixture to the freezer for a further 2–3 hours until almost solid.

3 Pour the apple juice into a small pan, add two cinnamon sticks and bring to just below boiling point. Pour into a jug (pitcher) and leave to cool, then remove the cinnamon sticks and set them aside. Chill the juice.

4 Spoon the cranberry ice into a food processor or blender. Add the apple juice and blend briefly until slushy. Pile into cocktail glasses, top up with chilled ginger ale and decorate with cranberries and a cinnamon stick.

600ml/1 pint/2½ cups chilled cranberry juice
150ml/¼ pint/⅔ cup clear apple juice
4 cinnamon sticks
about 400ml/14fl oz/1⅔ cups chilled ginger ale
a few fresh or frozen cranberries, to decorate

Serves 4

soft fruit and ginger cup

This wonderful combination of blended sorbet and ginger ale and vodka-steeped soft fruit makes a decadent treat. You will definitely need a spoon for this one.

1 Cut the strawberries in half and put them in a bowl with the raspberries, blueberries and sugar. Pour over the vodka and toss lightly. Cover and chill for at least 30 minutes.

2 Put the ginger ale and sorbet into a food processor or blender and process until smooth. Pour into four bowl-shaped glasses and add a couple of ice cubes to each glass.

3 Spoon a teaspoon of grenadine over the ice cubes in each glass, then spoon the vodka-steeped fruits on top. Decorate with the physalis and serve immediately.

115g/4oz/1 cup strawberries, hulled
115g/4oz/⅔ cup raspberries, hulled
50g/2oz/½ cup blueberries
15ml/1 tbsp caster (superfine) sugar
90ml/6 tbsp vodka
600ml/1 pint/2½ cups ginger ale
4 large scoops of orange sorbet
about 8 ice cubes
20ml/4 tsp grenadine
4 physalis, to decorate

Serves 4

Variation
To make a non-alcoholic version, use 90ml/6 tbsp orange juice in place of the vodka.

iced mango lassi

Based on a traditional Indian recipe, this drink is great with spicy food, or as a welcome cooler at any time of day. It is lighter and fresher than cream-based drinks.

1 To make the yogurt ice, put the sugar and water in a pan and heat gently, stirring occasionally, until the sugar has dissolved. Pour the syrup into a jug (pitcher). Leave to cool, then chill.

2 Add the lemon rind and juice to the syrup and stir well. Pour the syrup into a freezerproof container and freeze until thickened. Beat in the yogurt, then freeze again until thick enough to scoop.

3 To make each lassi, briefly blend the mango juice with three small scoops of the yogurt ice in a food processor or blender until just smooth. Pour into tall glasses and add the ice cubes, if using. Top each drink with another scoop of the yogurt ice, decorate with mint sprigs and mango wedges and serve immediately.

120ml/4fl oz/½ cup mango juice
2–3 ice cubes (optional)
fresh mint sprigs and mango wedges, to serve

For the yogurt ice
175g/6oz/¾ cup caster (superfine) sugar
150ml/¼ pint/⅔ cup water
grated rind and juice of 2 lemons
500ml/17fl oz/generous 2 cups Greek
    (US strained plain) yogurt

Serves 3–4

strawberry daiquiri

This decadent frozen cocktail blends rum and lime with fresh strawberries and strawberry ice cream to create a thick iced fruit purée.

1 Place the strawberries and the sugar in a food processor or blender. Process until smooth, then add the rum, lime juice and half the strawberry ice cream. Blend until smooth.

2 Scoop the remaining strawberry ice cream into four tall glasses and pour over the blended fruit mixture. Top up with chilled lemonade, decorate with fresh strawberries and lime slices, and serve immediately.

225g/8oz/2 cups strawberries, hulled
5ml/1 tsp caster (superfine) sugar
120ml/4fl oz/½ cup white rum
30ml/2 tbsp freshly squeezed lime juice
8 scoops of strawberry ice cream
about 150ml/¼ pint/⅔ cup chilled lemonade
extra strawberries and lime slices, to decorate

Serves 4

snowball

This iced version of the classic blended Christmas drink is enhanced with melting vanilla ice cream, zesty lime juice and spicy nutmeg.

1 Put half the vanilla ice cream in a food processor or blender and add the advocaat and the lime juice, with plenty of freshly grated nutmeg. Process the mixture briefly until well combined.

2 Scoop the remaining ice cream into four short glasses or tumblers. Spoon over the advocaat mixture and top up the glasses with lemonade. Sprinkle with more nutmeg and serve immediately.

8 scoops of vanilla ice cream
120ml/4fl oz/½ cup advocaat
60ml/4 tbsp freshly squeezed lime juice
freshly grated nutmeg
about 300ml/½ pint/1¼ cups chilled lemonade

Serves 4

hot-cold chocolate float

This unusual combination of steaming hot chocolate and ice-cold chocolate and vanilla ice cream makes a meltingly delicious shake.

1 Break the chocolate into pieces and place in a pan. Add the milk and sugar and heat gently, stirring with a wooden spoon until the chocolate has melted and the mixture is smooth.

2 Place two scoops of each type of ice cream alternately in two tall heatproof glasses. Pour the chocolate milk over and around the ice cream. Top with lightly whipped cream and chocolate curls and serve immediately.

115g/4oz plain (semisweet) chocolate
250ml/8fl oz/1 cup milk
15ml/1 tbsp caster (superfine) sugar
4 scoops of vanilla ice cream
4 scoops of dark chocolate ice cream
whipped cream and chocolate curls, to serve

Serves 2

coffee frappé

This creamy, smooth creation makes a wonderful alternative to a dessert on a hot summer evening. Use cappuccino cups or small glasses for serving.

1 Put half the coffee ice cream in a food processor or blender. Add the liqueur, cream and cinnamon and process briefly to combine. Scoop the remaining ice cream into four cups or glasses.

2 Spoon the coffee cream over the ice cream, then top with a little crushed ice. Sprinkle with cinnamon and serve immediately.

8 scoops of coffee ice cream
90ml/6 tbsp Kahlúa or Tia Maria liqueur
150ml/¼ pint/⅔ cup single (light) cream
1.5ml/¼ tsp ground cinnamon, plus extra
   for sprinkling
crushed ice

Serves 4

boozy blends

Frivolous and flirtatious or
sophisticated and elegant, blended cocktails
are the perfect choice whether you're winding down after
a hard day or winding up for a night of partying. This fun-filled
chapter offers a selection of cocktails that are sure to pack a punch
– from fresh and fruity to rich and creamy. Raise your spirits with a
glass of chilled blackberry and champagne crush or peach and mango
margarita or relax in your favourite armchair with a glass
of tomato-chilli punch.

peach and mango margarita

Adding puréed fruit to the classic tequila mix alters the consistency
and makes for a glorious drink that resembles a fruit smoothie
but packs considerably more punch.

1 Place the mango and peach slices in a food processor or blender.
Process until all the fruit is very finely chopped, scrape down the
sides of the goblet, then process again until the fruit forms a
perfectly smooth purée.

2 Add the tequila, triple sec and lime juice, process for a few
seconds, then add the ice. Process again until the drink is
quite smooth.

3 Pour into glasses, decorate with mango slices and serve.

2 mangoes, peeled, stoned (pitted) and sliced
3 peaches, peeled, stoned (pitted) and sliced
120ml/4fl oz/½ cup tequila
60ml/4 tbsp triple sec
60ml/4 tbsp freshly squeezed lime juice
10 ice cubes, crushed
mango slices, to decorate

Serves 4

tomato-chilli punch

This hot, peppery blend takes its inspiration from vodka-based Bloody Mary and Mexican Sangrita. You can use either vodka or tequila as both complement the fresh, spicy flavours perfectly.

1 Cut a cross in the base of each tomato and place in a heatproof bowl. Pour over boiling water to cover and leave for 30 seconds.

2 Lift the tomatoes out of the water with a slotted spoon and plunge them into a second bowl of cold water. The skins will have begun to peel back from the crosses. Peel off the skins, then cut the tomatoes in half and scoop out the seeds with a teaspoon.

3 Chop the tomato flesh and put in a food processor or blender. Add the onion, chilli, orange juice, lime juice, sugar and salt.

4 Process until the mixture is very smooth, then pour into a jug (pitcher) and chill for at least 1 hour before serving.

5 To serve, add the tequila or vodka to the tomato mixture and stir to combine, then pour into eight glasses.

450g/1lb ripe tomatoes
1 small onion, finely chopped
1 small fresh chilli, seeded and chopped
120ml/4fl oz/½ cup freshly squeezed
    orange juice
juice of 3 limes
2.5ml/½ tsp caster (superfine) sugar
pinch of salt
250ml/8fl oz/1 cup golden or aged tequila
    or vodka

Serves 8

blackberry and
champagne crush

This sparkling blend makes a good brunch alternative to Buck's Fizz. For a party, divide the blackberry purée among six glasses and top up with Champagne.

1 Put the blackberries in a food processor and process to a purée.

2 Place a sieve over a bowl and press the purée through the sieve to remove the seeds, then sweeten to taste with the sugar.

3 Pour the brandy into two glasses. Return the blackberry purée to the food processor, add the champagne or wine and blend for 2–3 seconds. Pour into the glasses and serve immediately.

175g/6oz/1 cup blackberries, chilled
15ml/1 tbsp icing (confectioners') sugar, to taste
30ml/2 tbsp brandy
250ml/8fl oz/1 cup Champagne or sparkling wine, chilled

Serves 2

blue hawaiian

This wonderfully over-the-top blended cocktail is a stunning shade of pale blue and should be served with a flamboyant decoration of colourful tropical fruits and leaves to really do it justice.

1 Pour the Curaçao, coconut cream and rum into a food processor or blender. Process very briefly until the colour is evenly blended.

2 Place the ice cubes in a dishtowel and crush to a fine snow with a wooden hammer or rolling pin.

3 Add the pineapple juice to the food processor or blender and process the mixture once more until frothy.

4 Spoon the crushed ice into a large cocktail glass or goblet. Pour the cocktail mixture over the crushed ice and decorate the glass with the fruit and pineapple leaves. Serve immediately.

25ml/1½ tbsp blue Curaçao
25ml/1½ tbsp coconut cream
45ml/3 tbsp light rum
3–4 ice cubes
45ml/3 tbsp pineapple juice
leaves and a wedge of pineapple, a slice of
    prickly pear or orange, a wedge of lime and
    a maraschino cherry, to decorate

Serves 1

Variation
Coconut and rum make a great base for any creamy cocktail. Try replacing the pineapple juice and Curaçao with 50g/2oz peach or strawberries and 25ml/1½ tbsp peach schnapps.

index

CONTENTS

THE SOCIETY OF SUPER SCIENTISTS

MAX AXIOM

After years of study, Max Axiom, the world's first Super Scientist, knew the mysteries of the universe were too vast for one person alone to uncover. So Max created the Society of Super Scientists! Using their superpowers and super-brains, this talented group investigates today's most urgent scientific and environmental issues and learns about actions everyone can take to solve them.

LIZZY AXIOM

NICK AXIOM

SPARK

THE DISCOVERY LAB

Home of the Society of Super Scientists, this state-of-the-art lab houses advanced tools for cutting-edge research and radical scientific innovation. More importantly, it is a space for Super Scientists to collaborate and share knowledge as they work together to tackle any challenge.

As the Society of Super Scientists answers an emergency call at the beach, they discover an even bigger problem. . . .

There's the bird we got the call about! It's caught in something.

Don't worry, I'll get you free.

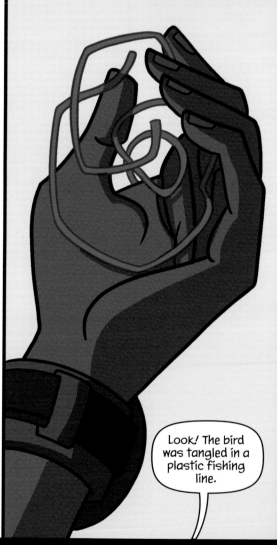

Look! The bird was tangled in a plastic fishing line.

SQUAWK!

Great job, Nick!

Look, Max! We're surrounded by plastic. It's in everything from sunglasses to cars, and even aircraft!

Plastic is a very useful material. It's strong and lightweight. It can be shaped into almost anything.

Plastic isn't a natural substance. Most plastic is made from oil, natural gas or coal. It was invented in 1869 but wasn't used much until after World War II. Then it started taking off.

In 1950, we created 1.36 million tonnes of plastic worldwide. In 2018, we made more than 317 million tonnes!

Unfortunately, people have come to think of plastic as disposable. Many plastic products are made to be used only once. Then people throw them away.

Some plastic is recycled, but not enough. In 2015, out of all plastic rubbish globally, only about 20 per cent was recycled.

When plastic is thrown in the bin, it ends up in landfills. Some landfills have special liners. They keep rubbish from spilling out into nearby land.

But if a landfill isn't built well, the rubbish leaks out. Not all countries have the resources to build effective landfills, either. So rubbish may be left out in the open or dumped.

It's also a sad fact that people litter. They just drop things like bottles, bags and sweet wrappers on the ground.

All that plastic is carried away by ocean currents. There are five main currents, or gyres, in the world's oceans. These whirling waters move lightweight plastic a long way from its source.

Plastic gathers in the centre of the gyres' spirals. That creates what are called garbage patches.

This research ship is studying the largest one. I'm sure Dr Reilly here can tell us all about it.

Welcome aboard, Super Scientists! Yes, we're out here learning about the Great Pacific Garbage Patch.

The Great Pacific Garbage Patch was identified in 1997. It's actually two large areas in the Pacific Ocean swirling with plastic debris. The Western Patch is close to Japan. The Eastern Patch is between Hawaii and California.

In 2018, the Eastern Patch was twice the size of Texas and weighed as much as 43,000 cars.

TRAVELLING DEBRIS

On 11 March 2011, a 9.0 magnitude earthquake struck off the coast of Japan. A tsunami followed. The disaster killed many people and caused billions of pounds in damage. It also washed an estimated 4.5 million tonnes of debris into the Pacific Ocean. Ocean currents carried the debris from the earthquake. The first plastic to reach North America was a football that washed ashore in Alaska in March 2012.

But I don't see much plastic out here.

People often think garbage patches are giant islands of plastic, but much of the debris isn't on the surface. You have to look *under* the waves.

We use this manta trawl to take water samples and learn what's in the ocean.

You see, plastic never really goes away. It just breaks into smaller and smaller pieces.

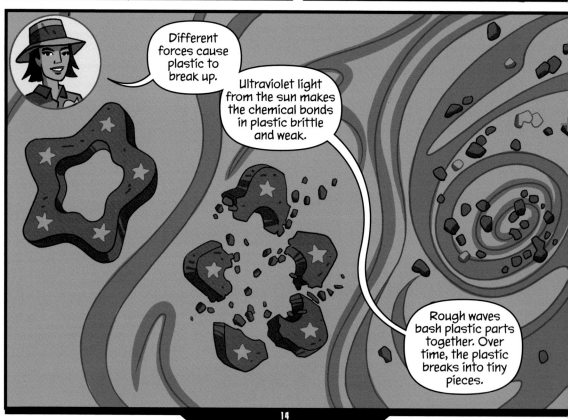

Different forces cause plastic to break up.

Ultraviolet light from the sun makes the chemical bonds in plastic brittle and weak.

Rough waves bash plastic parts together. Over time, the plastic breaks into tiny pieces.

We call these tiny pieces microplastics. The filter of the trawl catches them.

Microplastics make up over 90 per cent of the plastic in garbage patches. They float around under the ocean's surface. They're smaller than 5 millimetres, or 0.2 inches.

But microplastics don't have to break off from bigger plastic. Some are made that small, aren't they?

That's right. Microplastics are in toothpaste and soap scrubs. They even get rubbed off synthetic clothing fibres such as nylon or spandex in our laundry.

As plastics get smaller, the problem gets bigger.

I'm going to dive in for a closer look!

And soon, the fish end up on our plates.

Seafood is an important, nutritious food for people around the world.

But when we eat seafood, we are eating microplastics too. Scientists are still not sure how microplastics will affect us.

WARNING!
MICROPLASTICS
DETECTED

And 90 per cent of sea birds have eaten plastic.

They end up feeding plastic to their babies. Chicks can starve with stomachs full of plastic.

A 2014 study showed there were over 5.2 trillion pieces of plastic litter floating in the oceans.

That's about 700 pieces for each person on the planet!

And the problem is only getting worse. What can we do to protect our oceans?

I'm glad you asked.

Many people are looking for unique solutions to our plastic problem.

Dutch entrepreneur Boyan Slat was only 18 when he started The Ocean Cleanup.

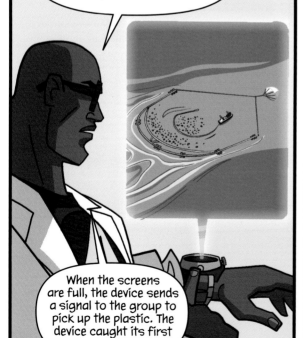

The group invented a net-like device to catch floating plastic. It gets carried through the ocean by waves and wind. As it moves, a large U-shaped tube gathers plastic on the surface. Screens hang down to catch plastic in the water.

When the screens are full, the device sends a signal to the group to pick up the plastic. The device caught its first plastic in 2019.

The Ocean Cleanup and other groups have also invented systems that catch plastic in rivers before it enters the ocean.

Hi, Super Scientists! I want to recycle the plastic I've collected. Can you help?

Of course! Recycling is one way to help cut down on plastic rubbish.

But it's important to know how to do it properly.

Many plastic household items have a number on them. This shows what kind of plastic it is.

Not all plastic items can go into the recycling bin. First, check what plastics your local recycling centre accepts.

Recyclables then have to be sorted by their numbers. They also have to be clean of food.

Okay, I'm ready to get to work. This bag can be recycled, right?

It can, but plastic bags clog the machines that sort plastic. So we can't put them in ordinary recycling bins.

PLASTIC TYPES

Not all plastic is recyclable. There are two main types of plastic: thermoset and thermoplastic. "Thermo" means heat. Thermoplastics can be melted and made into new products. Plastic bottles are thermoplastics. But thermoset plastics can't be recycled. Their polymer bonds won't change with heat. Plastic table tops and Formula 1 race cars are made from thermoset plastics.

We can't just recycle. To keep plastic out of the bins and our oceans, we also have to *reduce* and *reuse* plastic.

There are things we can start doing right away. You can say no to single-use plastics. Those are items such as plastic packaging, bags, straws and bottles.

An ice cream cone is better than a plastic cup! Tastier too.

Stop using plastic bags when you shop. Take a reusable bag with you instead!

TAKE ACTION!

Reducing plastic is a worldwide project. But you can start working on it now in your area.

- Plan ahead! Keep a reusable water bottle with you, have a set of utensils handy for on-the-go meals and carry a reusable shopping bag.

- Don't throw away plastic furniture or utensils. Donate them to a charity so that others can use items you don't need any more.

- Reuse plastic items for as long as you can. Clean plastic takeaway containers and reuse them. Grow plants in a plastic milk carton. Then water them with a watering can made from a clean plastic laundry detergent bottle.

- Get creative! Think of new uses for plastic items. Find out what plastics your council recycles. Make sure you always recycle those items.

- Write to your local government and ask them to help increase recycling in your schools and community. Encourage friends and neighbours to do the same.

- Start a poster campaign in your school or local area. Use it to teach people about why it's important to reduce, reuse and recycle plastics.

- Pick up plastic in your area. If you can recycle it, do it! If not, cleaning up litter keeps it out of our streams, rivers and oceans.

- When you are shopping, try to buy products with no packaging or recyclable packaging. If you can, shop at a farmer's market or community market. Buying local usually means less plastic packaging.

- Try a plastic-free challenge! Can you go through a day without using plastic?

MORE PLASTIC FACTS

Some scientists think the plastic rubbish floating near the ocean's surface is only 1 per cent of all the plastic in the ocean. Recent studies found that there is far more plastic on the ocean floor than is floating near the surface. In 2018, a piece of plastic was found in the Mariana Trench at 11 kilometres (36,000 feet) deep!

Plastic is found all over the world – even in places where humans don't live! Microplastics have been found in the snow in Antarctica. On uninhabited islands such as Milman Island, near Australia, plastic is ruining what should be beautiful beaches. Sea turtle researchers collected more than 75 kilograms (165 pounds) of plastic from the shore.

Scientists and businesses are working on creative alternatives to plastics. One company in London is developing a plastic made from seaweed. This plastic is not only biodegradable – it's edible!

Scientists in Korea may have discovered a beetle larvae that can eat, digest and break down a specific kind of plastic called polystyrene.

GLOSSARY

disposable made to be thrown away

gyre large system of rotating ocean currents

landfill place where rubbish is buried

litter rubbish that has been thrown on the ground or carelessly left somewhere

manta trawl netted device that is pulled through water to collect water samples

microplastic piece of plastic less than 5 millimetres (0.2 inches) long; microplastics can either be purposely made in a small size or they are pieces that have broken off from large plastic items

monomer single molecule that can be linked to other molecules

plastic strong, lightweight material created by people that can be formed into many shapes when heated and then set as it cools

pollutant material that can damage the environment

polymer group of many monomers linked together

recycle make used items into new products

reduce make something smaller in size or quantity

FIND OUT MORE

100 Things to Know About Saving the Planet, Various (Usborne Publishing Ltd, 2020)

Guardians of the Planet: How to be an Eco-Hero, Clive Gifford (Buster Books, 2021)

What A Waste: Rubbish, Recycling, and Protecting our Planet, Jess French (DK Children, 2019)

WEBSITES

www.bbc.co.uk/newsround/42810179
Learn more about why plastic in the oceans is such a huge problem.

www.dkfindout.com/uk/science/materials/plastics/
Find out more about plastics with DK Findout!

INDEX